MW01225878

Awkward Guy

Poems and other embarrassing things

by Franco Bertucci

Drawings by Erwin Dence

Poems ©2016 Franco Bertucci   Drawings ©2016 Erwin Dence

To my family

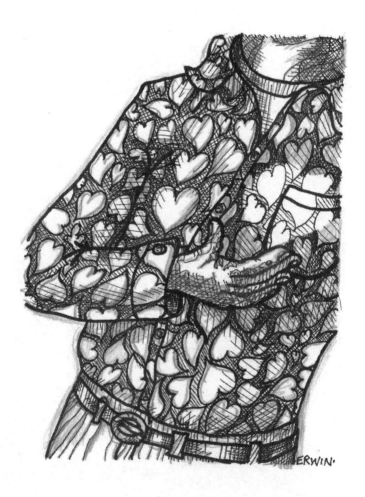

Contents

Jazz Mosquito

Jazz belongs in the city
where the light is dim
and the background noisy
and life a bit more confusing.
Where being smart is a sport.

Jazz is good when you want to think,
but not about something.
When you want to feel
aloof and to wallow, both at once.

Jazz bespeaks balance
and being very good,
knowing it and caring.
It never states the obvious,
is wary of making statements at all,
is rich and wandering
and self-indulgent. Jazz is exhausting.
But, each note is a charming surprise
if you are one of the few
who can follow them.

One can dig it, one can
learn to breathe the stuff.
But there are places it can never go.
There are beautiful places
away from the city
where you don't hear jazz,
and if you do, you want to swat it.

I Could If

I know I could conquer the world
if I could just stay on task
for more than a minute
without getting side-tracked
by more interesting pursuits-
such as conquering my wife
and children.

Nothing Messes Up an Artist

Nothing messes up an artist
like saying you like his stuff.
After that, he can never be the same.
After that, you'll be in his head.
Every time he makes a new one,
he will worry that you won't like it.
After that, he will analyze everything,
try for repeat performances.
He will be haunted by the thought:
I was better before.

Guardian Tower Angels

Through the age of baby fat
our children have guardian angels that
protect their towers made of blocks
from the laws of physics.

Later in life, the last block
will always topple the tower- but not now.

Angels who take pleasure
in a little guarding recreation
after a long day of averting disaster
are the only reasonable explanation.

I Want Something

I want something.
I thought it was beer.
It isn't.
I try the next aisle
and the next.
Champagne is the only thing that looks good,
but I don't want to pay for champagne, tonight.

I came into this store because I want something,
but deep down I know
no one sells what I want.

That won't stop me from trying my luck
with some cookies.

The Rooster

I am a rooster,
or a cock,
according to the place mat
at your local Chinese restaurant.

Basically,
that means I am a genius,
along with Eric Clapton.

Sun Day

Forget snow days.
School should be against the law
on a day like today.
Teachers should go on hikes
and pick berries.
Children should ride bikes
and blow through the kitchen for lunch,
then ride to the neighbors' house
for another lunch.
On a day like today they need to work
on their physical and cognitive development
and resistance to dirt-borne germs.
A child can make great strides
on a day like today,
or wither in a classroom.

Why Hurricanes Were Named After Women

They used to name hurricanes after women
and fathers who have daughters know why,
and if I were a woman, I'd be flattered

To be associated with a beautiful force
no man can handle, or understand,
but can only watch in awe-
while holding onto something.

If it were up to me,
we would still name hurricanes after women only
and blame ourselves for the wreckage.

But, if there were a need to balance things out,
we could name mud slides after men.

My Favorite Thing to Step On

Somewhere between me and the glass of water
I will retrieve for my love
There lies waiting
For my bare left foot
In the dark,
A plastic toy goat.
He has come all the way from China for this.

Order Out the Window

I have forty-seven miles of road
left as a passenger in this van
in which to figure out my life.
After that I will have no time
for such frivolous pursuits.

God help me.

I've tried this before and failed.
It is so easy to look out the window
and let my thoughts fly
in no particular order, whatsoever.

A New Mess

A blank page.
An empty calendar.
A vacant stage.
Also-
undeveloped property for sale,
studios for rent,
a nicely made bed.

Clean, orderly and ready to go-
beginnings are the best.
Very alluring is
the idea of making
a brand-new mess.

Go to the Ocean

Go to the ocean and forget your troubles.
They will seem small, compared to the ocean.

Birds of the Air

All of my interior struggles were needless
today, I have decided.
Whatever problems and obstacles
I thought I was confronting
the whole day long,
were dissolved this evening
by several fish tacos and a beer.

Actually, two beers.

Once again, I had overlooked the basics.

The birds of the air neither reap, nor sow,
nor waste time on interior struggles
and they remember to eat when they're hungry.

To Catch a Mole

She sits by the mound and waits
intently, quietly and nothing
ever happens while I am looking.

It's amazing to me
that moles can be caught.
This creature that I have never
glimpsed in action
I find lying, bought,
at the bottom of our porch steps:
A gift, or something like that,
from an incredibly patient cat.

What wild things might I catch,
if I could focus like that?

Mangia Mangia

After a very long plane ride
we got to Italy
and I got mad at dinner
because I was relaxing
and you were studying grammar.

I am sorry I got mad
and I am sorry my Italian
is not better.

Obvious Secret Knowledge

The ancient Egyptians had secret knowledge
and so did the Mayans
and the Aztecs
and so does my Grandpa.

And when he dies
he will take most of it with him-
because he doesn't know it's secret.

Godless Poets

Many poets sense they are doomed.
Some take this on the chin
and write with good sportsmanship,
not wishing to make anyone's doom
worse than it needs to be.
And perhaps it won't be so bad, for them.

I have a feeling the others,
when they go to hell,
will be reading a lot of poetry.

Bad Beavers

She got up the other morning
to find her two favorite plum trees,
not robbed of plums,
not injured by beetles,
not scarred by a weed-whacker,
not pruned to death by the power company,
but simply gone-

Stolen by some local beavers
who needed a couple of sticks.
Of all the inconsiderate things.

I Want to Waste Time

I want to read a spy novel.
I want to fly a space ship
into danger.
I want to study chess and
play it on Thursday nights,
Pinochle on Wednesdays.
I want to kiss my wife
at eleven in the morning
to keep us both from working.
She wants to practice archery-
on horseback.

I want to deliver a letter
to someone far away, by sailboat.
I want to listen to records,
smoke cigars, sip drinks and talk.
But I don't tend to sip.

I want to waste time
but I don't want to feel
like I wasted time.

Not by Request

Hie thee hither, kiss me
and then hie thee home and wait for me
with a candle lit and a bottle open
and a warm plate covered with a napkin.

I did not tell you any of this,
but this is the way it happened.

She Fights With Her Sweater

She fights with her sweater
and the sounds of the struggle
echo through the house.
We listen and await
the consummation of the battle.

Sometimes the sweater wins
and father rushes
to free her from the bonds
of the wily sweater.

Sometimes the sweater loses and no one cares
as, once again, it silently bears
the humiliation of being stretched inside-out and backwards.

Can't Waste a Handsome Face

A good-looking man I know,
(he knows he is good-looking,)
lit on fire the college theater
and made the stage manager cry.

I guessed he would end up famous.

Now he arrests people,
writes tickets for a living
and you can bet still makes people cry
with his striking face and fiery soul
and the fact that he is taking them to jail.

I understand his reasons, and probably,
he is right.

Still, he has at least one true fan
selfishly hoping for his comeback to art.

If You Know Chickens

Some days we run around like chickens
with their heads cut off.

But if you know chickens you know that is not the worst.

Some days we run around like chickens
with their heads still on.

Reckless Typewriting

Hero: You want me to hang myself? There's no reason for it.

Famous Author: There's no reason for anything.

Hero: Then you have no reason to protest
as I tie your hands to your desk
and drop this quality typewriter on your fingers.

The Un-strange Thing

I won't ask how it happened,
for I think I have a pretty good idea.
And I won't ask where the time went,
for fear that a physicist might tell me.

Everyone knows that life is strange,
but I want to know
how we know that.

Where is the un-strange thing we compare life to?

Drunk People Dancing

Drunk people dancing
and sober people thinking about it.
The lights casting shadows
and the band getting deaf
feeling good
forgoing the details
which get blurry in situations like this
aware of a warm cosmic something
a boat perhaps
which all of us are in-
even the people who aren't here
the loves at home
and the dead people from history

They don't hear all the words
when they're dancing like that
but they catch a few
and feel the arc of each song
the troughs in between
and I know we're communicating
with the sober people too
even if it's a little primitive-
this is pop music after all

Death to the Machine

My friend says
it's ok to hate a thing,
if not the person who made it.
The same friend once set his up in the backyard
and shot it.
And buried it.

But I'm pretty sure he has a new one now.

Worried About Someone

when you're worried about someone
and suffering because you haven't heard from him
and the message you hear when you call
never ever changes
and you think he should have been here by now,
a long time ago actually,
and despite the existence of all these devices
which send signals to space and back
to help us stay in touch
you hear nothing
and know nothing
and so can do nothing
but pray
and get on with life
like they must have done in the days
when letters took six months to cross the ocean

but at night, when you have time to worry again
you lie awake and think of all the dreadful things
that may have happened to keep him away

and when he suddenly shows up- in one piece at that,
you spank yourself for having had no faith at all;
for this has all happened before

I Have Made You Lopsided

"Look at what you've done to your wife."

I have made you lopsided
and it's hard for you to roll over in bed
or slide behind the wheel.
Sometimes I feel guilty about it.
But I am not the one
who arranged things this way.
I'll take my turn when the time comes.
In the meantime, you are beautiful
and I am filled with tender, fatherly feelings-
like fear.

Stealth in the Morning

I practice stealth in the morning
But the stealth of a ninja is useless
Against the senses of a two-year-old
Whose instincts arouse her
Always just in time.

Un-supervised parents. Downstairs.
About to accomplish something useful.
No. Worse.
Attempting romance.

The Color Dreary

"The sky is not dreary; the sky is gray,"
protested the girl to her father,
who was grateful to be rescued that morning
by his daughter of forty-two months,
from passing the whole day
mistaken in his colors.

Suffering for a Woman

My wife puts her cold feet on my back
and I do not scream
but take it like a man
and reflect- how lucky I am
to suffer in this fashion
for a woman.

But tonight,
my feet are cold.

Proper Goodbyes

When the party's over
at the end of the night
my mind always goes straight
to the one person who left
before I got to say hello
or goodbye.

Free Range Eggs

Scratch, scratch in the dirt
for worms, for grubs, for bugs
to eat and make into lovely eggs
that we could have for breakfast;
if we could only find them.

Let's Break our Brains Thinking About Time

I quote George, from my sixth grade class:

"The present is the shortest amount of time possible,
but there is no shortest amount of time possible."

Thank you, George. And now let us move on
to calculating the universe's mass.

Mini Mart

All he said was,
"You need coffee?"
and I knew that he was good
and that we would
be fast friends-
brothers-
were I to stick around.

Perhaps every traveller
who caught his open sign
at three in the morning
felt the same about him.
Any live being
you meet at that hour
is your friend by default-
if he has coffee.

I've had warm feelings
in mini-marts before.
Convenience store clerks
are a gentle race-
in contrast
to the junk they sell.

But this man, I think,
was an angel sent to the Highway 2 Mini Mart
for some disguised, important reason-
brewing coffee, mopping the floor
and listening for a signal.
But I couldn't stay
to find out anything more.

Guilty Catholic

Guilt is a big part of my life.
But that's not a bad thing.
The truth will set you free,
and the truth is, I'm guilty.

Still, I'd rather not get into specifics.

Girl Trouble

My father's explanation is simple:
It's because she is female
and she is two years-old,
but mostly, because she is female.

Somehow this doesn't comfort me-
you jaded old man.

To Do List, March 29, 2011

~~hug children~~
~~kiss wife~~
~~saw boards~~
~~pay bills~~
~~write poem~~
go to post office and find surprise check for $10,000
go to bank
go home
kiss wife
hug children

You Look Good in the Snow

You look good in the snow.
Don't deny it.
It just so happens I know
you are the descendant
of a Norwegian princess.

Spirited to Bed

I wish there were a peaceful way
of extracting children from cars
and transporting them to bed, asleep.
But there are too many buckles,
noisy doors,
and changes of temperature
on the path.
But if I could spirit them to bed,
there might be some hope
of spiriting you to bed.

Pooh

Trouble on two legs
scuffs down the stairs,
into the kitchen pushes a chair,
puts his hand in the honey,
just like a bear.

Belittled Somehow

There are clever ways of hiding
the importance of a thing.
A crafty thinker thinks of them
and calls your beloved faith
a "belief system."

Sleep Reading

I have been working on a new skill, in the evenings.
It is called sleep-reading.
Since marriage and children
I have mastered sleep-talking
And sleep-listening.
And I can sleep-read to myself,
Pages and pages, comprehending not a word.
But I know I have yet to master
Sleep-reading aloud
When my daughter slaps me mid-story,
Detecting that the plot has gotten terribly off course:

Little Red Riding Hood sharing bread and jam
With a big, bad badger named Albert.

You Don't Know When You're Good

You don't know when you're good
or why people love you.
But I do.
So have fun
and leave the editing to me.
I will cut out the bad.

You won't be able to see it
but to me and everyone else
it will be obvious.
I will do my hacking when you're not looking.

Don't try to be good
or to guess what I am going to like.
Because I don't know till I see it-
and you won't know even then.

If I had a self-forgetfulness pill
I would give it to you.
Actually, I do have one
but it has the side-effect
of making you drunk.

It won't do
to make a habit of that
on a project like this-

but we might use it in a pinch.

About the Author and the Illustrator

Franco Bertucci is a music teacher and performer who has been on the road a fair amount and been at home more. He wrote many of these poems while building a house for his young family and discovering, among many other things, that writing poems is quicker than writing songs. Franco lives in an exciting little town on the Olympic Peninsula of Washington State. Write him at: awkwardguy@gmail.com

Erwin Dence is a house painter, painting contractor, writer and surfer. He lives in the same exciting little town as Franco but has been there a lot longer. Erwin is one of the reasons Franco can describe the place as exciting. To see more of Erwin's artwork and writing, visit realsurfers.net, or his blog, "Stuff That Goes On" at ptleader.com.

Thanks

To Mario, Scott and Toni for telling me my poems were good, after happening across them when I wasn't looking.

33485472R00035

Made in the USA
Middletown, DE
15 July 2016